MW00976649

MISSISSIPPI IN ᴍᴇ

Copyright, 2016 by Patricia Neely-Dorsey

All rights reserved. No part of this book may be reproduced in any form without written permission from the publishers, except by a reviewers and authors, who may quote brief passages in a review to be printed in a book, newspaper or magazine.

ISBN: 978-1-944583-08-8

For copies of this book, contact:

Patricia Neely-Dorsey

1196 CR 681

Saltillo, MS 38866

(901) 848-6800

E-MAIL: magnoliagirl21@yahoo.com

WEBSITE: www.patricianeelydorsey.com

This book is published by Laurel Rose Publishing, 1930 Holston Rd, Como, MS 38619

TEL: 662-612-0703

WEBSITE: www.laurelrosepublishing.com

Printed in the UNITED STATES OF AMERICA

3

Faulkner's Sanctuary
Eudora's Elvis'
home state birthplace
THE BULK OF THE TRACE

Sprawling beaches
Along the Gulf Coast shore
ONE BLUES MAN'S CROSSROADS
And inspiration for more
An abundance of history
Tradition and folklore
Warm front porch welcomes
With a wide open door
A ride down the mighty river
ON THE AMERICAN QUEEN
And some of the most
Beautiful countryside
THAT YOU'VE EVER SEEN
She's music and melodies
And the mockingbird's songs
By valor and arms And faith ever strong
She's magnolias blooming
Around Jackson's capitol dome
And the sweet scent of honeysuckle
That forever says "home"
She's my Mississippi She's "The Hospitality State"

"Go Mississippi"
You're a true State
of Grace

Table of Contents

INTRODUCTION

There are so many negative connotations associated with Mississippi and the South, in general.

Through my poems, I attempt to give a more positive glimpse than usually portrayed.

I invite readers to "Meet Mississippi and the South Through Poetry Prose and The Written Word," Always, Always Celebrating the South and Promoting a Positive Mississippi "

DEDICATED TO

My Mississippi, With Love

M ississippi means Great River or Mighty Waters

I t has been nicknamed the "Hospitality State"

S inging The Blues started in the Delta

S avory tamales can be found on each plate

I t houses the headquarters of the Natchez Trace

S ince most of it run through this place

S weet magnolias bloom all around

I t's often called "The Magnolia State"

P eople everywhere have heard Elvis sing

P erhaps they don't know that our Tupelo

I s The Birthplace of "The King"

Mississippi

MEET MY MISSISSIPPI

Faulkner's Sanctuary
Eudora's home state
Elvis' birthplace
The bulk of the Trace
Sprawling beaches
Along the Gulf Coast Shore
One blues man's crossroads
And inspiration for more;
An abundance of history
Tradition and folklore
Warm front porch welcomes
With a wide open door;
A ride down the mighty river
On the American Queen
And some of the most
Beautiful countryside
That you've ever seen
She's music and melodies
And the mockingbird's songs,
By valor and arms
And faith ever strong;
She's magnolias blooming
Around Jackson's capitol dome
And the sweet scent of honeysuckle
That forever says "home"
She's My Mississippi
She's the "Hospitality State"
"Go Mississippi"
You're a true State of Grace

MISSISSIPPI WELCOMES YOU

Mississippi welcomes you,
With wide open arms;
Here we let our hospitality show,
And exude southern charm.
We welcome you to the Birthplace of Elvis,
The Cradle of Rock and Roll and the Blues,
The home of some serious home-cooking,
And some famous Blue Suede Shoes.
Come sit a spell on our front porch,
Sip some delicious sweet tea;
Chat about one legendary blues man,
And that Crossroads mystery.
Take a scenic drive,
Down the Natchez Trace;
Catch dinner from a catfish pond.
Let us introduce you to the works,
Of our literary greats,
Of whom we are so fond;
Spend some time on the sprawling beaches
Along our Gulf Coast shore;
Sample award-winning seafood,
That will certainly have you begging for more.
We have so very much to offer here,
You'll want to visit year after year;
And when you have to leave us,
You might even shed a tear

MY MISSISSIPPI

M y Mississippi

I s always home to me

S he's warm, charming and alluring

S he's the queen of hospitality;

I 've loved her from my earliest days

S he's in my fondest memories

S he's in my heart, in my soul and such a part of me

I love to share her beauty,

P eople often misunderstand;

P leasures abundantly abound,

I n my dear magnolia land.

MISSISSIPPI

In the heart of Dixie,
Perfumed by
The sweet, fragrant smell of magnolias
And serenaded with
The melodious songs of the mockingbird,
Lies a true Queen of the South.
Her name is Mississippi.
I don't know how to explain this place,
Except to say that she "speaks" to me.
The rocks, the flowers, the birds and trees
Speak to me.
They sometimes whisper,
And sometimes they shout;
But always they say,
"This is where you belong."

MISSISSIPPI LOVE

She is the apple of my eye
Continually
She has made me who I am
Quite Favorably
She is flawed, I know
But, not fatally
I do love her, still
Most Passionately

A MISSISSIPPI HAIKU

Much misunderstood
Still, she whispers sweet welcomes
In her gentle breeze

M FOR MISSISSIPPI

Music
Melodies
Mockingbird Songs
Magnolias and Memories
My Home Sweet Home

A MISSISSIPPI HOME

Lots of Cooking
Lots of Eating
Lots of Friendly neighbor greetings
Lots of Praying
Lots of Singing
Lots of Sunday-Go-To-Meetings
Lots of Love
Lots of Laughter
Lots of Front porch swings
Lots of Stories
Lots of Memories
Lots of Sweet, Simple things

HOME
(Sweet Home Mississippi)

Like a bird in a feathered nest,
Or a rabbit in its burrow
Your brilliant sunlight
Embraces, warms and comforts me
Your gentle breezes
Whisper softly in my ear
And lull me to sleep;
I cannot tell the particular thing
That makes me know
That you are the only place for me
And with you is where
I always want to be
All I know is
Everything about you
Says...
"Home"

MADE IN MISSISSIPPI

Along with...
Syrupy, sweet hospitality,
Down home,
Delta blues,
And beautiful
Magnolia girls;
Strong family values,
Unbreakable bonds,
And lifelong memories
Are Made in Mississippi.

MISSISSIPPI MAN

I want to enjoy my Mississippi Man
On a Mississippi day
Soaking up some Mississippi sun.
I love the way we do Mississippi things
And have our Mississippi fun.
He makes me laugh a Mississippi laugh,
And smile a Mississippi smile;
And, I guess, if he would ask me to,
I'd run a Mississippi Mile.

MISSISSIPPI MORNING

I love a Mississippi morning,
On a summer's day;
Everything's so glorious,
In the most delightful way.
The sun is peaking upward,
The earth begins to warm;
Magnificent works of nature,
Are simply just the norm.
There is a sense of wonderment,
At how all things look so new;
The flowers glow with freshness,
From the past night's dew.
The beauty all around you,
Would take away your breath;
You'd feel you'd like to soak it in,
Until there's nothing left.
There's nothing like a Mississippi morning,
On a summer's day;
It's such a grand production,
It seems we all should pay.

IF MISSISSIPPI'S IN YOU

If Mississippi's in you,
It'll always be that way;
It matters not how far you go,
Or how long you stay.
If Mississippi's in you,
It always plays a part
In how you live and move and breathe,
And in every notion of the heart.
If Mississippi's in you,
It's in you through and through;
It's in who you are and how you be,
And it's in everything you do.
If Mississippi's in you,
There is some special glow;
A different something down inside,
That all the home folks know.
If Mississippi's in you,
It'll always be that way,
From the time you enter in the world,
Till in the grave you lay.
Every true Mississippian,
Can surely have it said
I'm Mississippi born,
I'm Mississippi bred,
And when I die,
I'll be Mississippi dead.

HAPPY BIRTHDAY MISSISSIPPI

Happy Birthday, Mississippi
Queen of the South
True Jewel of the Southland
Your grand attributes we tout
You have birthed literary greatness
And musical genius abounds
In your mystical trove
Where endless treasures are found
Your Grace, Charm, Hospitality
And warm caresses we crave
Yearning for your gentle breezes
From the cradle to the grave
You are always with us
And no matter how far we roam
Your sun-drenched land of magnolias
Will forever be our home
With much love we honor you
Though much misunderstood
Your strong ties bind us to you
And we look only to the good
We all sing your praises
And raise your proud banner high
Pledging steadfast allegiance
Until the day we die.

MISSISSIPPI THROUGH AND THROUGH

I could not be more
A part of the Mississippi landscape,
If I had sprouted right out of the soil
In some farmer's garden,
Or bloomed from a magnolia tree
In the yard of some plantation home,
Or emerged, like Venus,
From the murky waters
Of some catfish pond.
I feel Mississippi.
I think Mississippi.
I move Mississippi.
I breathe Mississippi.
I am simply,
Mississippi through and through.

REFLECTIONS OF A MISSISSIPPI MAGNOLIA

When I look back on my life,
I think how wonderful it has been;
To have had the most
Wonderful parents of all,
And a host of wonderful friends.
My high school days were blissful,
And my college days so fun;
Fond memories are one thing for sure,
That I have by the ton.
I'm so glad that I grew up,
On Mississippi sod,
My t-shirt reads: "American by birth,
And Southern by the grace of God."
My life has been so wonderful,
I wouldn't change one condition;
As one friend of mine always says,
I should have paid admission.

MISSISSIPPI MAGNOLIA

Home is where the heart is,
That's what they always say;
Well, my heart is Mississippi's
In the most profoundest way:
It's who I am,
It's what I like,
It's everything to me;
A Mississippi Magnolia girl
Is all I'll ever be.

MISSISSIPPI HAS MY HEART

I always knew I was in love with her
I could not help but be.
Warm gentle breezes blowing softly,
Through thick canopies of trees
Along endless, winding country roads.
Sunlight dancing on rippling waters of
Secluded catfish ponds,
Moonlight casting a magical glow
Across Delta fields
Overflowing with dazzling white
"Mississippi Snow"*
Tall sprawling oaks casting long shadows
Over grassy clover-filled meadows
And roots reaching deep into my soul.

*Mississippi Snow = Cotton

Magnolia

MADE IN MAGNOLIA

I'm made in Magnolia
I'm Mississippi strong
I'm so proud to say Mississippi's home

I'm Made in Magnolia
It's my heart and my soul
The joys that she's brought me
Will never grow old;

I'm Made in Magnolia
And it's not hard to see
Mississippi, forever and always,
Lives inside me.

MUD AND MAGNOLIAS

I'm simple, sweet, southern
Living life close to the earth
I'm mud and magnolias
And that way since birth.
I thrive on front porches,
Sweet tea and tire swings
I adore the country, rustic
Uncomplicated sort of things;
I'm that barefoot and carefree
Exploring back roads type of one
With no need for extravagance
For my kind of fun
I'm mud and magnolias
And so proud of that fact
I'm sweet, simple, southern
And so glad to be just that.

MOONLIGHT AND MAGNOLIAS

Sweet, warm welcomes
Whisper in her gentle breeze
A voice heard quite clearly
Lingering among the trees
She beckons all to know her
A comforting, southern den
Enter in her borders
Explore the joys within.

MAGNOLIA LOVE

Sweet, Southern Magnolia Love
Is like a lazy barefoot walk
Down a country road
With cool earth slipping between your toes
A romp in cool clovers
Under a cloudless summer sky
And soothing raindrops
Tapping rhythmically on an old tin roof
During a cleansing spring shower.
It's like the magical glow of lightning bugs
In the dark still night
And a long day on the riverbank
When the fish are biting just right.
It's an earthly, rooted, grounded
Forever kind of love.

THE MAGNOLIA TREE

There's a majestic, old magnolia tree,
That stands in my front yard;
It's a tree that's grown there for ages,
And whose beauty you can't disregard.
She spreads her branches quite nobly,
And her stance is that of a queen;
She stretches her arms so commandingly,
As if certainly crying out to be seen.
She's the center of much activity,
And I know a squirrel family lives there;
I'm sure she affords them much comfort,
For her branches don't ever go bare.
There's so much that's gone on around her,
I'm sure that so much could be told;
But, she keeps all her secrets well-guarded
And, simply, remains a sight to behold.

MAGNOLIA BLOSSOM

She is a delicate flower
Dressed in white, like a blushing bride.
Open wide with possibility;
She is the epitome
Of southern charm and grace.
Her admirers stand in awe,
Of such a perfect creation.
Her fragrance is intoxicating,
Her beauty...
Timeless.

THE MAGNOLIA

She speaks to me of
Romance
Elegance
Charm
And Grace
A genteel maiden
Perfect gift of the southern sun
Blowing kisses in the wind.

MISS MAGNOLIA

A magnificent creation
Dressed in snowy white
Lovely to behold
A captivating sight
You grace us
With your presence
Countenance like a queen
Such a stately lady
Beauty evergreen.

I AM MAGNOLIA

Do you see me?
I am
Large, Showy
Magnificent
Beautiful milky white
A flawless creation
Product of the southern sun
Fragrance like no other
A wonder to behold
I want you to love me
But...
You must handle me with care.

STEEL MAGNOLIA

Breathtaking,
Delicate beauty
Of creamy perfection
With roots running deep
In southern soil,
A history almost
As old as time,
And endurance
As tough as steel
She defies description
And explanation
But....
Beauty is its own excuse.

Mississippi

Magnolia

Southern

SOUTHERN LIFE

If you want a glimpse of Southern life,
Come close and walk with me,
I'll tell you all the simple things,
That you are sure to see.
You'll see mockingbirds and bumblebees,
Magnolia blossoms and dogwood trees,
Caterpillars on the step,
Wooden porches cleanly swept;
Watermelons on the vine,
Strong majestic Georgia pines;
Rocking chairs and front yard swings,
June bugs flying on a string;
Turnip greens and hot cornbread,
Coleslaw and barbecue;
Fried okra, fried corn, fried green tomatoes,
Fried pies and pickles, too.
There's ice cold tea that's syrupy sweet,
And cool, green grass beneath your feet;
Catfish nipping in the lake,
And fresh young boys on the make
You'll see all these things
And much, much more,
In a way of life, that I adore.

SOUTHERN MAN

There's nothing like a Southern man,
He's a man that you should know;
He's one to whom you'll find no equal,
Anywhere you go.
He has a sweet molasses talk
And a slow, smooth gliding walk.
He's got strong firm hands that let you know,
Real work is nothing new;
He has no problem with the fact,
That he should provide for you.
There are certain kinds of values
This man is sure to hold
His love of home and family
Is sure to not grow cold.
He'll deeply love his mother
It's a bond that's always there
All throughout his life, this man
Will show her tender care.
He's one that you can count on,
To do the manly things;
He'll change the tire and check the oil,
And fix the backyard swing.
But, underneath a tough exterior,
A gently soul lies too;
He's one who'll rock the baby,
And even cook a meal or two,
On Sundays, he'll sit beside you singing,
On the same church pew.
There's nothing like a Southern man,
He's a rare and special kind;
If you look forever, anywhere,
He's the best you'll ever find.

LOVE LETTER TO THE SOUTH

My Dear South
You have captured my heart
And captivated my mind
With your sweetness, your charm
Your hospitality, your grace;
Your gentle breezes whisper softly in my ears
And soothe something deep inside
Your radiant sun wraps around me like a cloak
And warms my very soul
You give me comfort
And peace
And joy;
You are
My sanctuary
My refuge
My home
I cannot imagine me
Without you
Though many don't understand...
I have loved you
And will love you
Always and Forever.

SOUTHERNERS KNOW

Southerners Know
Of a special place
With warm, gentle breezes
And sun on your face.
Southerners Know
Of home-taught rules
And simple graces
That they never lose.
Southerners Know
Family, Friends and Faith
Are deeply cherished,
And hold a deep-seated place.
Southerners Know
No matter how far they roam
It's a southern life on southern soil
That will always be home.

FRONT PORCH

(Hospitality Headquarters)
Just the spot
For taking in a cool breeze
And watching the world go by
Friends and neighbors out
For a leisurely stroll
Stop and sit a spell.
"Lemonade?"
"Iced Tea?"
"Co-Cola?"
"Did you hear about...?"
"Do Tell!"
"You Don't Say!"
"My, how the time flies"
"Y'all come back, now"
"You hear?"

YARDSALING

Yardsaling is a southern art,
And to some it's a way of life;
It's a way of getting almost anything,
Without the stress and strife.
You meet all kinds of people,
And you see how others live;
And while the kids sell lemonade,
You negotiate what you'll give.
There's always a faithful crew,
That gets up before the dawn;
To see what treasures they might find,
On some neighbor's lawn.
There's much anticipation,
Of the next bargain 'round the bend;
And everyone knows in yardsaling,
The possibilities never end.
There's always something
You've been searching for,
Suddenly, staring you in the face;
And when your eyes lock on to it,
Your heart begins to race.
There's nothing like the yard sale game,
Or should I say, the sport;
It quite easily becomes an addiction,
If you're of that sort.

THE RULES

Most Southern folk have rules we're taught,
From when we're very young;
And most of us, throughout our lives,
To these rules have clung.
Life can be much easier,
When you know what to do or not;
And you're sure to learn a lot of them,
If Southern parents you have got.
One of the first rules you come to know is
Children are to be seen and not heard;
It's best if you just sit down somewhere
Quietly as a bird.
You always say "Please" when you're asking.
And "Thank you", when you receive;
You address all your elders
As "Ma'am" or "Sir",
And if you don't do it, you'll grieve.
Don't touch anything in the store,
Keep your hands to yourself;
If it's not something you plan to buy,
Leave it soundly on the shelf.
Always say "Good Morning",
Soon after you awake;
And always greet people pleasantly,
If friends you are to make.
Don't slam a door as you walk out,
"You don't live in a barn,"
You'd better close it gently,
Is what they'd always warn.
If you open a cabinet or anything,
Always close it back;

Once you do it repeatedly
You'll always have the knack.
Don't call someone before 8 a.m.,
Or after ten at night;
If it's something you feel you must do,
It's an urge that you must fight.
Never ask for food when you visit,
Although the host may ask;
Sometimes it's best if you decline,
And let the moment pass.
These are just a very few of the things,
We Southerners are taught;
Without some rule for every occasion,
We are never caught.

BOTTLE TREE

They say
That evil spirits
Are captivated by your beauty
As you stand glistening in the sun.
Wanting a better look,
They come closer
And get caught.
That's what
They say.

BACKROADS

Rocky,
Dusty,
Bumpy,
Curving,
Twisting,
Turning
Tree-Canopied pathways;
The Short cut
The Scenic Route
Or the long way home.

NICKNAMES

"What's his name?"
"Who?..
Pee Wee,
Peanut,
June Bug,
Dimp, Shine,
Bird, Snake, Rat,
Shortie, Buddy, Bubba, Mack?"
"Yeah...
But, what's his real name?"
"Beats me..."
"We just always call him...
That."

SOUTHERNERS REMEMBER

Southern folks remember when
All of the stores in town
(except maybe a few gas stations)
Closed on Sundays...
Everyone went to church
And the preacher was always invited
To someone's house to eat after services.
We remember when
Cars pulled off to the side of the road
As a funeral procession passed...
And when the whole "village"
Really DID help raise the child.

49

VARIOUS SUPERSTITIONS

I must admit we Southerners
Are a superstitious lot
And some can be quite serious
About the beliefs we've got.
"Don't walk beneath a ladder,"
"Don't step on a sidewalk crack;"
"You're best to go around it,
Or you'll break your mother's back;"
"Don't let a black cat cross your path,"
Or let a broom sweep across your feet;
Don't ever break a mirrored glass,
Or bad luck you're sure to meet."
The old folks would say
"Remember these things,
And hold on to them fast;
If you neglect anyone of them,
Your good times sure won't last.

WHERE I'M FROM

I'm from magnolias and dogwoods and
sprawling farm lands
I'm from walking down dirt roads and
"Do what you can"
I'm from banana pudding and peach
cobblers at dinner on the grounds
I'm from country, gospel, Elvis rock,
and that Delta Blues sound
I'm from Easter Sunday shiny
black patent leather shoes
And from those "No White After
Labor Day" strict set of rules
I'm from "Don't You Sass Me"
and "Hush Yo' Mouth"
I'm from that beautiful, mystical,
magical place called... "The South"

Country Life

COUNTRY LIFE

In the country,
I was a no shoe girl
With hair wild upon my head;
I'd run and play and make mud pies,
Until I went to bed.
There were chickens and cows,
Goats and pigs,
Animals all around
And somehow, everything we did,
Was connected with the ground.
We'd root around in the garden
And go fishing in the pond;
We'd pick wild berries on the path,
And have all kinds of fun.
We'd walk along the dusty roads
And eat the red clay dirt;
In the country, we always knew,
"A little dirt could never hurt".
I truly lived a country life,
That's plain for all to see;
It was a unique way of life
But one so right for me.

COUNTRY LIFE

It's grassroots.
It's simple.
It's basic, not plush.
Uncomplicated,
Uncluttered,
Unhurried,
Unrushed,
It's relaxed,
Unpolluted,
Unequaled,
Unmatched.

SWEET TEA AND SUNSHINE

I was raised on sweet tea and sunshine
With bare-feet and winding dirt roads
I ate my food straight from the garden
And drank water from an outdoor hose
I am used to the sound of screen doors
slamming
And crowing roosters at the crack of dawn
I enjoyed wide open spaces
With a pasture instead of a lawn;
I loved my country upbringing
And it's still in me from my head to my toes
I was raised on sweet and sunshine
And I share so that everyone knows.

LET'S

Let's go for a ride in the countryside,
And make lots of stops along the way,
Let's soak in all the warm sunshine,
And create a perfect day.
Let's stop at someone's roadside stand,
And maybe buy some fruit;
Let's pretend it's some great find,
Just like a pirate's loot.
Let's go inside a country store,
And have some bologna cut;
Let's sit outside and eat our fare,
Like some treasure from King Tut.
Let's always enjoy life's simple things,
And to their full extent;
Let's always spend these kinds of times,
And make it our intent.

YOU AIN'T COUNTRY

If you've never...
Swept the front yard (No, not the porch but the yard),
Played under the porch (Yes, under)
Intentionally eaten dirt
(Not just any dirt, mind you, that good old red clay kind)
Gone barefoot outside...all day
And seen old car tires used as
Flower planters and yard decorations and swings...
You ain't country.
If you've never...
"Sopped" syrup or gravy with a biscuit
Shelled the peas for your supper or
Drank coffee from the saucer
You ain't country.
If you don't know what a truck patch is
Or about the grease can on top of the stove
Or that canning vegetables
Does NOT involve a can...
You ain't country.
If you've never used a mason jar as a drinking glass
Or to eat milk and bread from
Or to cut out homemade biscuits with.
You ain't country.
And if you're not shaking your head in agreement
And smiling a bit as you remember...
I know for sure
You ain't country.

YOU AIN'T COUNTRY (PART 2)

If you've never...
Had...
Big fluffy homemade biscuits
With syrup and mashed up butter
Or sausage gravy Or streak of lean (strick-o-lean)
Yes just a streak of lean pork meat
And mostly fat...fried to a crisp
For breakfast...
You ain't country.
If you've never...
Eaten...
A mayonnaise sandwich
Or ketchup sandwich
Or a thick tomato sandwich
With salt and pepper
And juice running down your fingers
On a hot summer day
You ain't country.
If you've never had...
Turnip greens or mustard greens or collard greens
Served with a big chuck of raw onion on your plate
Or hot cornbread crumbled up in just the juice...
Pot liquor (Pot likker)
You ain't country.
And if you are not nodding...
And maybe licking your lips
Just a bit I know for sure...
You ain't country.

YOU AIN'T COUNTRY (Part 3)

If you've never put peanuts in your Coca-Cola
Or had a moon pie
on the back porch with a tall RC
Or eaten "Nabs" with a cold Nehi drank (Yes,
drank, not drink)
You ain't country.
If you don't know about
Chunkin' rocks or
Totin' water or
Spitting watermelon seeds
To see whose will go the furthest
You ain't country.
If you can't look out in an open field
In the summertime
And readily point out some "rabbit tobacco"
Or a "snake doctor"
You ain't country.
If you don't know what it means
When someone says I'm just piddlin' (an activity)
or I'm fair to middlin' (state of being)
You ain't country.
If you've never seen an old LADY (yes, lady) Dip
snuff...
Or pull out a coin purse from her bosom
To give you some money
You ain't country.
And if you're not smiling just a bit
And maybe letting out a little chuckle
As you remember I know for sure...
You ain't country.

GOOD EATING

A thick tomato sandwich
Bursting with flavor
Peppered to taste
With a watermelon cut
Straight from the vine
Are nature's bounty
In a country life
In the summertime

TALKIN' (COUNTRY) SOUTHERN

Well I'll be!
Lawd a mercy!
How y'all doing?
We ain't seent y'all in a month of Sundays
How's yor mama and 'nem?
Won't y'all sit a spell?
We was jus' fixin to go to the store...
To make groceries
But it look like it's coming up a cloud
I reckon we best wait till that blow over
That last storm pert near blew us clean away
Our mailbox ended up way over yonder in
That pasture,
Who that you got wit' y'all?
Oh that's Johnny's boy!
He know he the spittin' image of that man!
He sho done growed.
He kinda favor his cousin, Joe, too.
That Joe ain't got a lick of sense.
Bless His Heart.
That whole family used to live right up
That road a piece
We know all his people.

COUNTRY BREAKFAST

A real country po' folk's breakfast
Is in these days quite rate,
It's certainly not your typical
Bacon and eggs type affair.
There'd be crispy fried chicken,
With all the parts there to eat;
The usual ones represented,
Plus the neck, back and feet.
There might be some country ham,
But not the thin, sterile kind;
It's the thick, salty slices
From the smokehouse you'll find.
If you're lucky, there's rabbit,
From a recent hunt trip;
With juicy, brown gravy
That drips from your lips.
There would probably be rice,
With sugar and butter of course;
And big chunky biscuits
That could choke any horse.
What goes in the middle,
Is anyone's guess;
Some molasses or syrup
Would sure pass the test.
But, most want preserves
From the cook's vast store;
From the past summer's canning,
In flavors galore.
The milk would be powdered,
And straight from a box:
There's likely no juice,

'til opportunity knocks.
But, we all know one thing
That's sure to be had;
It's a jug full of Kool-Aid,
And the flavor is
Red.

HOG KILLING TIME

There's a chill in the air
And holidays are near;
Thanksgiving's just 'round the bend;
There's a feeling amongst country folks
That's absolute prime,
Everyone senses its hog killing time.
Oh what a spectacle!
Oh what a show!
You'll find nothing like it,
If you look high and low.
From sunup to sundown,
It lasts the whole day;
And once it gets started,
Horses couldn't pull you away.
Everyone has his own part to do,
With all the commotion,
It feels like a zoo.
The poor victim for this occasion
Has long been picked out,
And soon will become food,
From his tail to his snout.
There's a shot and a squeal
And he's out for the count
A cut of the throat,
And blood spews like a fount
In a barrel of hot water,
He's cleaned and de-haired;
Amongst all the men,
This giant task is shared.
A skillful knife separates all parts of meat,
Including pig ears, pig tail, and pig feet.

The women's task is always chittlin's to make.
There's a boatload of goo and muck
They must rake.
When nighttime falls,
All surround the black pot;
Where the oil is bubbling,
And boy is it hot!
Pieces of skin are stirred with a surge,
And after some time,
Crisp cracklings emerge.
Sweet potatoes are roasted,
Right in the fire;
And of these simple treats,
No one ever does tire.
When it's all finally over,
And the day is all done;
The grown-ups are weary,
But the kids just had fun.

SHELLING PEAS

It's summertime in the country,
And the kids buzz around like bees;
But, when that silver tub is placed on the porch,
It's time for shelling peas.
From the smallest to the oldest,
It's something we'd all do;
At first, of course, the little ones,
Didn't have a clue.
They'd watch to see just how it went,
And soon, they'd give a try;
Then, look amazed at fingers stained,
As though dipped in purple dye.
When we'd first get started,
It seemed an insurmountable chore;
There looked like half a million peas,
Or maybe even more.
But, after we all got the flow,
We'd turn it into fun;
We'd have a race to see just who
Would be the first one done.
We'd each one have our own bowl,
And a paper sack;
We'd slip our fingers through the hull,
Then throw it empty back.
At last, when all the shells lay empty,
And a tub of peas was done
We'd let the grownups take the haul
Then look for some new fun.

Tupelo

WELCOME TO TUPELO

We welcome you to Tupelo
With wide open arms
Here, We Let Our Hospitality Show
And exude southern charm
We invite you to the Birthplace of Elvis
And the headquarters of the Natchez Trace
Discover the history and heritage
In abundance, in this place
Learn all about Mill Village and Chief Piomingo,
Shakerag,
The National Fish Hatchery and more
Find the place where "The King" got his first
guitar
At our very own Tupelo Hardware Store
Visit the Oren Dunn Museum
With our proud past displayed at its very best;
Sample a true southern delicacy
At the annual Dudie Burger Fest
Explore our First TVA City
Nestled in the Mississippi Hills;
Those looking for fine dining and shopping,
Can certainly get their fill.
Take in a show at the Lyric Theatre
Or try the Gumtree Run
Tour this All-America City
And find all kinds of fun
See amazing cars at the Automobile
Museum
And, exotic animals at the Buffalo Park
You'll discover that there are endless adventures
On which anyone can embark

Let us show you the Tupelo Spirit
Which is, forever shining bright
Streaming out from Northeast Mississippi,
As a true beacon light.

THE TUPELO SPIRIT
(Tupelo, MS)

Heartily embracing history and heritage,
Past and present
Forging faithfully forward
And celebrating a rockin', rollin' native son
In the beautiful Mississippi Hills;
Always helpful,
Always hopeful,
The Tupelo Spirit shines bright

THE KING
Elvis A. Presley

(Born: Jan 8, 1935, Tupelo, MS.)

From poor and meager beginnings,
A young man began to sing;
From the small town of Tupelo,
A voice began to ring.
As surely as it's been said,
A man's gifts make a way for him;
This humble diamond
In the rough,
Became a sparkling gem,
Velvet melodies and Explosive rock,
Were the gifts he'd bring;
The world responded
With resounding praise,
And pronounced this man "The King"

THE BIRTHPLACE

Would anyone have suspected
The stories that these walls held
Of a mother working fingers to the bone
And a father who was jailed?
All the secrets that lived inside,
The world would not have known;
If the young man with the old guitar
Had not ascended to his throne.
Would anyone have wanted to know
About the family from "across the tracks,"
Who could hardly keep food on the table
Or clothing on their backs?
Would anyone have even cared,
About the heartaches, pain and scorn
If this tiny frame house hadn't found acclaim
As the place where "The King" was born.

SHAKERAG

Even in the shadows of Shakerag,
They came through;
They sang
They danced
They laughed
They loved
Nothing could quench
Indomitable spirits Dishearten
Determined souls
Or Discourage
Made up minds
Emerging from the shadows of Shakerag,
They thrived.

Childhood

REMEMBER

Remember
When "Going to Memphis"
Was a really BIG road trip
And vacations meant
Howard Johnsons and Stuckey's
Remember
When people got excited
About simple things
Like homemade ice cream
Church picnics
And
Softball games
Sunday drives
And the county fair
I remember those things
Do you?

BUS RIDE

Trailways
Greyhound
Across the Mason-Dixon Line
To see Country Cousins or City Kin
Fried Chicken and
Biscuits, Bologna and
Cheese And Crackers
Tucked away for the ride
Crumpled paper sacks as
Lunch bags and luggage
Jingling change for emergency calls "Stations"
and stops
Often old country stores
And road side stands
Or..
JUST the dusty road
"There seems like a million stops!"
"This could take forever!"
"I hope we get there soon."

EASTER

Easter bonnets and baskets
Ruffled socks
And greased up legs
Hair all curled up tight
Patent leather shoes
With a biscuit shine
And everyone all astir
Ready for the Easter "parade"
Children, Church and Chicken dinners
Speeches and the hunt
"Easter Easter it's so sweet
I forgot my Easter speech"
"What you looking at me so hard for?
I didn't come to stay.
I just came to let you know,
Today is Easter day".

FAIR DAY

Out of School
Free Admit
Hanging with "the gang"
Let's all meet at Long's Laundry
Is the plan that's made
Lights flashing
Bells ringing
People calling out "Try this one"
"Step this way"
"You'll win without a doubt"
We ride...
The Bumper Cars
The Tilt-A Whirl
And a few more favorite things
We pick up ducks,
We throw the darts
And casually toss the rings
With Corn Dogs, Cotton candy
Funnel Cakes and lemonade
The money's spent, the day is made.
Heading out
There's always time
For that one last game or spin
"Guess my weight?'
"I bet you can't!"
"That's not it!"
"I win!"

UNDERSTOOD

Growing Up...

We all knew

THE   Store

THE   Corner

THE   Shortcut

THE   Hiding Place

THE   Candy lady

and ...

The   Rules

Times Past

SUNDAY DINNER

Sunday services over
And the dinner table set
A prominent place
At the head of the table
For the preacher as a guest
Mother scurries all about
And shoos the kids away
"Don't touch a thing!"
"Behave yourselves!"
"Go somewhere and play!"
Fried chicken, mashed potatoes,
String beans and more
Properly laid out
Then, a knock at the door
Daddy takes the preacher's hat
Mother beams with pride,
"Do come in!"
"We're so glad you came!"
"You kids...
Go outside!"

THE ROLLING STORE

Friendly merchant

With puttering truck and ready smile

Travels down Miles and Miles

Of winding roads

And grassy pathways;

Faithful customers

Anxiously await

As he uncovers his load

Of needed items

And, always, hopefully,

New delights

CAREFREE

Running through clovers
In a flour-sack dress
Sun on her face
Warm breeze in her hair
Looking up and wondering
What really lies beyond those clouds
Not a care in the world
For this sweet,
Barefoot, southern child

(Un)MODERN (In)CONVENIENCE

Winter Time.
Late Night
Gotta Go !
Outhouse?
Too Cold.
Too Far.
Nightpot.

SEEING

In my mind's eye
I see the children playing,
People walking, talking,
Living, laughing, loving
Like they used to
In days gone by
Forever changed
And still changing.
I see the houses,
The spouses,
The families
The neighbors,
And the "hoods"
Vibrant and alive
On landscapes now laid bare
Is it a gift or a curse?
I wonder.
I still see, feel, remember it all
Do you?

ANCESTORS

Up from the land the ancestors call
Remember us they say
Remember our toils and our trials
Carry us with you day by day
Seek to find the old pathways
Remember the old landmarks
Never forget from whence you've come
As on life's journeys you do embark
Cherish our stories and lessons
Hold them ever dear
In all of your remembrances
We are kept forever near

Music

THE DELTA

Flatlands stretch endlessly
Toward the horizon
As far as the eye can see;
Rich, black soil
Yields endless rows
Of blinding white wonder
On fertile ground
That gives birth to the blues.

THEM BLUES

Some body's always singing
Them Monday Morning blues songs
Them sho' nuff done me wrong songs
Them stayed out all night long songs
Them moaning, groaning love songs
Them bare your heart and soul songs
Them feel it in your bones songs
Them make you weak and strong songs
Them letting go and holding on songs
Them everybody knows songs
We ALL love them blues...songs

BLUES MAN

Filling up the room,
Invading the senses
With Brooding,
Moaning,
Groaning melodies
Of Hurt and Heartache
Love and Loss
Stolen Kisses
Deep Longings
Deep Passions
Deep Pain;
Blood, Sweat and Tears
Drip from his fingertips
Through his instrument
And straight to the core of our souls.

REAL "SOUL MUSIC"

When I sing those
Old songs of Zion
My mind goes back to
Jesus "At The Cross"
And how "HE Bore It All"
TO take away my sins
Now, in the church,
He can "Hide in the Blood"
I "Thank You, Lord"
That I have "A Friend Like You".
One day "I'll Fly Away"
And "I'll Live In Glory"
"Oh I Want To See Him"
"Just Over In The Gloryland"
So I must,
"Hold To God's Unchanging Hand"
To receive my "Mansion, Robe, and A Crown"
And see those "Hilltops of Glory"
"Won't It Be Wonderful There"?

Seasons

A TASTE OF SPRING

Birds Singing
Grass Greening
Colors Blinging
Nature's Springing

RENEWED

Winter winds chill us
Yet, the Spring brings a new hope
All life is renewed

(SOUTHERN) SUMMER SUN

Streaming Rays of Beaming Light
Gleaming Rays of Dazzling Bright
Is the Southern, Summer Sun

SUMMER NIGHT (SOUTHERN STYLE)

Moths flicker 'round the front porch light
Fireflies are taking flight
The sun has disappeared from sight
And all around the sound of night.
Everything is warm and still
A sense of calm that one can feel
The moon shines bright over yonder hill
Can all this loveliness be real?

SOUNDS OF SUMMER

Chirping of the crickets
Buzzing of the bees,
Bullfrogs croaking in the pond,
Birds singing in the trees:
These are sounds of summer
That we all wait to hear,
It's part of what's so wonderful,
About this time of year.

FALL (IN THE COUNTRY)

Floating to the ground
Like delicate snowflakes
And crunching underfoot
With each movement
Autumn leaves blanket the ground
In dazzling shades
Of red, yellow, orange and gold.
A deer darts through the woods
As hunters await.

FALL LEAVES

Each fall leaf tells a story,
Yielding a lesson
Of the circle of life
Changing,
Evolving,
Falling
And dying;
To be renewed
In another season.

Thanks

DR. KING

Dr. King, we thank you
For taking a stand
And for fighting injustice
All through the land.
We appreciate you implementing
Your non-violent plan,
Seeking equality
For every man.
Changes have come,
That have benefited many;
And the challenge remains,
To leave out not any.
The struggle continues
To make it clear
That everyone's rights
And freedom are dear.
May we never forget
To honor your dream
And seek those ideals,
No matter how hard it may seem.
We look to your example
In leading the way
To a brighter future.
And a much better day.

MAYA

Thank you for gifting us
With your unique rhythm, beat and flow
Helping us to fully appreciate
That womanly glow
Encouraging us to speak boldly and sing
Without fear's dark spell
For we each have a song
And a story to tell.
Because of you so many
Rise and stand proud, seek to lift others up
And be a "rainbow in the clouds"
Thank you for teaching us
To reach further to think and to grow
And to do the better thing
Once we know.
Thank you for showing us
How to thrive and to "Be"
And how to live out our lives
Phenomenally.

THANKS, MOMS!

A special thanks goes to every mother,
From every daughter and son;
Remembering and appreciating you,
For all the things you've done.
You've supported and encouraged us,
To dream and reach so far,
You've always helped us to believe,
That we could reach that farthest star.
We thank you for protecting us,
From our own selves, sometimes, it's true;
And always being there to give wise counsel,
As just a small part of all you do.
Thank you mothers for blessing us,
With a love strong fast and true;
There could never be words in all the world,
To express what's owed to you.

THANKS, MOM AND DAD

I love you Mama and Daddy
You taught me oh so much;
I can't begin to describe all the ways,
That my life you profoundly touched,
You taught me morals and values
You helped me reach my goals
And all things I learned from you
Will stay till I am old.
I want to thank you deeply,
For being there for me;
And for being absolutely, without a doubt,
The best parents ones could be.

NATURE LOVERS

My dad would teach me of nature,
He'd point out all of the trees;
And as we walked around in the yard,
He'd help me recognize all the leaves.
Looking out of our windows
He'd name all the birds there for me;
If an especially pretty one happened by,
He'd make sure that I'd see.
To this day I'm thankful,
For all of the insights he gave to me;
I think of them with every beautiful sunset
That I see
I try to pass all this along,
To my only son;
I want him to notice all of God's works
And appreciate everyone.

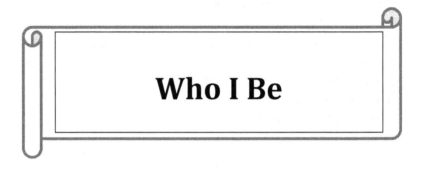

Who I Be

WHO I BE?

Who I Be?
I Be Me.
But, there's much more to me,
Than the me you see.
I can be sunlight and laughter
Or Storm clouds and rain;
I might cry when I'm happy
Or even laugh when in pain.
I am sometimes the anchor
And sometimes the sail
I'm often successful,
But sometimes I fail.
Sometimes,
I'm Exactly
What you think, hope, want
Or expect me to be;
But Most importantly,
I Be Me.

BEING ME

Call me what you want to,
I only answer to my name;
It might seem meek and lowly,
But it's my only claim to fame.
Being me is all I know,
And no one can do it better;
Every aspect of the task,
I have down to the letter.
Who I am, inside and out,
Is really all I've got;
I want to be the best of me
And never who I'm not.

THE FRINGE

I've always lived life
On the outskirts
I've always lived life
On the fringe
Always a little too much of this
For most folks
Always not quite enough of that
For the crowd
I smile to myself
And just have to say
That I really, really think
I like it that way.

THOSE EYES

An old faded portrait
Familiar features
A steely gaze
And a hauntingly beautiful face;
The eyes look out at me
Across time and space;
Those eyes tell a story
Of great courage, dignity and strength
Sorrows, sadness and pain
In those eyes I see a proud legacy
And deep inside those eyes
I see
Me.

BE YOU! DO YOU! SHINE!

Listen to your own muse
Heed your inner voice
Follow your Dreams
Pursue Your Goals
Firmly Stay the Course
Let your light
Lead the way
As I will do with mine;
Lovingly embrace
All that you are
Be You!
Do You!
Shine!

PND

Who?
PND?
You mean that...
Poem writing
Positive spouting
Mississippi Magnolia
Five dollar dress wearing
Diva on a dime
Chick?
Yeah.
That's her!
That's
ME!

FLAVOR

I've got flavor.
Like jazz music…
Which they say is
A perfect blend
Of musical styles
That makes that smooth
Intoxicating, soulful sound
And like a delicious gumbo
Which takes lots of
Relatively ordinary ingredients
Mixed together to make
An extra ordinary dish
I've got flavor.
It takes a perfect combination
Of a little bit of this
And a little bit of that
A pinch of this
And a pinch of that
Put together
In just the right way
To REALLY have flavor.
I've got flavor.

Love

THE SOFTER SIDE OF LIFE

You are an old fashioned man
I'm an old fashioned girl
We want to live
In an old-fashioned world
We want the softer side of life
Without the harsh cold edge
Where man and woman intertwine
Without some competitive wedge
We look for easy, quite times
In all the things we do;
With jazzy tunes and full lit moons
And hectic moments few.
We like a slower, measured pace.
No rushing here and there;
We like to stop and smell the roses
And take the utmost care
We like the little niceties
That others push aside
We like the little courtesies
And from them do not hide
We notice all the little things
As we go along our way
A dazzling sun
A crisp white sheet
A blade of glass beneath our feet
A knowing glance
A sparkling love
Are things that we hold dear
And we both feel certain
That things are better
When the other one is near.

IT SEEMS

Did I know you
Before I knew you
Before we met?
It seems like I did
Did you speak to me
Before you first spoke to me
Before you ever uttered a word?
It seems like you did
Are our minds on some shared frequency
And our hearts connected by a single cord?
Are our souls somehow fused together
And the sums of our parts
Simply meant to come together
To make one perfectly complete
Beautiful whole
I am not sure
But....
That is certainly the way
It seems

OUR PLACE

There is a place of enchanted love,
Where only you and I do dwell;
It's a place that's quiet and warm and safe,
A place that none can tell.
It's a very special private place,
A place that no one knows,
It's a place where we do find our rest,
A place of sweet repose.
It's a place of tender kisses,
Of knowing hearts and minds,
A place of wonderful delights,
And marvels of all kinds.
It's a place where we move in a timeless rhythm,
To the beat of our own drums;
It's a place where emotions flood our souls,
And to which we must succumb.
It carries us through a time and place
Where love can never end;
A sacred place that's so divine,
Where man and woman blend.
It's a place I want to dwell forever...
Just you and me alone;
A solemn place where love is shared,
Like none has ever known.

THE DANCE

Magic flows between the two.
Measured advances,
Turns and twists
Excite and Electrify;
Movements executed
Carefully,
Thoughtfully
Seamlessly
With precision
Harmoniously blend
Making their own sweet music.

THE WEDDING

Not a dry eye is in the house
With tears of
Happiness,
Joy,
Excitement,
Anticipation,
And some with a twinge of sadness
Along with lots and lots of ones for...
If they only knew.

HONEYSUCKLE DREAMS

You are, somehow, always near to me
Though we are far apart
I keep you ever close to me
In spirit and at heart
You go with me throughout my days
And especially through my nights
You invade all my senses
And make my thoughts take flight
You are, somehow, always near to me
Though often far apart
For I see you
And I feel you
And even touch you
It seems...
In my sweet, sweet
Honeysuckle dreams

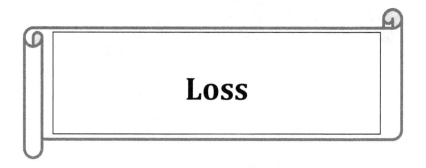

Loss

SEASONS OF LOVE

It's been winter between us
For too long
Cold, barren
Dormant and
Unyielding.
I shiver
Seeking warmth.
It has been winter between us
For too long
Do you even remember the spring?

IN THE MIST

I can see (it) (us)
But not clearly
Everything is
Fuzzy,
Unclear,
Mysterious
Mystical
What's in store...
For me...
For us...
I can't tell
It's all
In the mist

GONE TOO SOON

Your light was among us
Shining
So brightly...
Brilliantly;
So splendidly
You were
Dazzling
Amazing
White Hot
Then...
Suddenly...
So sadly...
You're Gone...
Too Soon

THAT DAY

Mama does laundry in the big black pot
On a beautiful day in the
Spring Churning, turning the boiling water
The clothes will be so clean
There's a gentle breeze in the air
The wind whistles all around
The fire is fanned hotter, hotter
And leaps higher from the ground
Baby runs and plays, nearby
In her own little world, you'd guess
Such a pretty little thing
Darting all about
In her cute little flowered dress
Suddenly, too close to danger
Her hem is all aflame
Tragedy strikes on this cloudless day
And nothing is ever the same
Hurt so badly
With a burn so deep
It's not long before the child is dead
The doctor's just "weren't no count"
Her grieving mother said

* From account told to me by my great-
grandmother about the loss of her daughter.

THE STORM

A crystal blue sky
And cloudless day
Show no indication
Give no signs
How you came through
And wreaked havoc;
Changing the landscape
Of our lives
Forever.

FINDING ANSWERS

Tears fall
Hearts ache
Many questions
Much confusion
So much pain ...
How do we...
Go on?
Forgive?
Find mercy?
Find love?
Find hope?
It's faith that answers all.

CPSIA information can be obtained
at www.ICGtesting.com
Printed in the USA
JSHW012349160919
1495JS00001B/1